cozy crochet

cozy crochet

26 fun projects from
fashion to home decor

by melissa leapman
photographs by france ruffenach
illustrations by randy stratton

CHRONICLE BOOKS
SAN FRANCISCO

Text copyright © 2004 by Melissa Leapman
Photographs copyright © 2004 by France Ruffenach
Illustrations copyright © 2004 by Randy Stratton

Library of Congress Cataloging-in-Publication Data available.

ISBN: O-8118-4079-4

Designed by Vivien Sung
Styling by Aaron Hom/Zenobia
Typeset in New Century Schoolbook, Neutra, and Memimas
Manufactured in China.

Distributed in Canada by Raincoast Books
9050 Shaughnessy Street
Vancouver, British Columbia V6P 6E5

10 9 8 7 6 5 4 3 2 1

Chronicle Books LLC
85 Second Street
San Francisco, California 94105
www.chroniclebooks.com

for marla and daniel

I'd like to thank the following talented crocheters who assisted me with sample making and pattern testing for this book: Brenda Allred, Marianne Forrestal, Sara Gillingham, Cindy Grosch, Marty Miller, JoAnn Moss, Laura Polley, Michele Posner, Tina Posner, Barbara Pretzsch, and Sharon Ryman.

I am especially grateful to the many yarn and button manufacturers who have supported my work throughout the years and have supplied materials for this project.

Thanks, too, go to Mikyla Bruder and Chronicle Books for suggesting this book to me. Together, we'll introduce the wonderful world of crochet to a whole new group of crafters!

table of contents

introduction

The craft of crochet is truly magical!

Some folks consider it an art form. Others find it a practical and fun craft. For all, it is a technique that allows us to transform soft, shapeless balls of yarn into beautiful and useful objects for ourselves and for others.

Crochet has become more popular in the past several years. Trendy crocheted garments are showing up on fashion runways all over the world. They're featured in nearly every ready-to-wear catalog and department store collection. And pretty crocheted laces remain a staple in the home decor industry.

The biggest surprise about crocheting is that it is not only fun but also easy to learn. With very little investment in tools and materials, you can have a hook in your hand, happily looping away in no time!

Early sections of this book will lay the groundwork for a lifetime of crocheting, introducing you to the tools of crochet, all the basic stitches, and every technique you'll need in order to get started. The first set of projects—Everyday Dishcloth and Soft Coaster—are suitable for absolute beginners. You'll get the hang of crocheting without having to worry about the evenness of your stitches. But, like most crocheted pieces, the results are beautiful and practical, too!

In all, I've designed twenty-six fun-to-stitch projects for this book. Both beginners and experts will have much to choose from here, since projects for a wide range of skill levels are included. And, for additional creative inspiration, each project includes a "Variation" suggestion to help you put your personal spin on your creations. Surely, once you pick up your hook and yarn, you'll never want to stop!

Happy Crocheting!

chapter

getting started

supplies

yarn

What a wonderful time to learn to crochet! Manufacturers and spinners offer an incredible variety of materials for crocheting, from beautiful silky cottons to warm, fuzzy wools, to soft, machine-washable acrylics. The way a crocheted fabric feels is as important as the way it looks, so experiment with lots of different fibers—and materials—as you learn. For variety, I've included projects using thread and lace as well as some unexpected materials—fabric strips and even metal wire—in this book.

hooks

Hooks are the basic tools of crochet and can be made out of many materials. Their circumference determines the size of your crochet stitches. Smaller hooks yield smaller, tighter stitches; larger hooks create larger, looser ones.

Strong steel hooks are typically used with fine yarns or thread. They range from size 14 to size 00. Hooks with smaller numbers have larger diameters.

Lightweight aluminum, plastic, and wooden hooks are generally used with yarn. They range in size from B to K, with circumference size increasing with each subsequent letter of the alphabet. Some manufacturers make hollow plastic hooks as large as size Q or even size S, which are great for quick-to-stitch projects using super-bulky yarn!

miscellaneous supplies

You'll probably want to assemble a crochet tool kit for yourself—a special box or canvas bag to hold your current project(s) as well as the following useful items:

Sharp scissors

Tape measure

Blunt tapestry needles
   with large eyes

Safety pins

Straight pins

Stitch markers

Row counter

how to read a crochet pattern

Crochet patterns may seem like they're written in a secret code or foreign language when you first see them. Have patience with yourself as you learn the vocabulary. Always read the entire pattern before beginning any project. A list of abbreviations and crochet conventions follows.

abbreviations

approx - approximately

bb-sc - back bead single crochet

beg - begin(ning)

ch(s) - chain(s)

ch sp - chain space

cont - continu(e)(ing)

dc - double crochet

dec - decreas(e)(ing)

dec dc - decrease double crochet

dec hdc - decrease half double crochet

dec sc - decrease single crochet

dtr - double triple crochet

FPDTR - front post double triple crochet

hdc - half double crochet

inc - increas(e)(ing)

LH - left hand

mm - millimeter(s)

mult - multiple

oz - ounce(s)

patt(s) - pattern(s)

quad tr - quadruple triple crochet

rem - remain(ing)

rnd(s) - round(s)

RH - right hand

RS - right side

sc - single crochet

sp(s) - space(s)

st(s) - stitch(es)

tog - together

tr - triple crochet

tr tr - triple triple crochet

WS - wrong side

yd - yard(s)

conventions

* - an asterisk means that you need to repeat instructions after asterisk or between asterisks across row or for as many times as instructed

( ) - parentheses indicate that you need to repeat instructions within the parentheses for as many times as instructed, *or* are used to indicate a set of stitches to be worked all within one stitch or space, *or* are used to indicate various alternative sizes, with the number preceding the parentheses referring to the smallest size and changes for successive sizes shown within them

[ ] - brackets are used to indicate a set of stitches to be worked all within one stitch or space

turning-ch (turning chain) - the number of chain stitches used to bring the yarn and hook up to the height required in order to work the next row

work even - continue crocheting in pattern as set, without increasing or decreasing

foundation row or round - the first row or round of a piece of crocheted fabric

american vs. british terms

American terms are used throughout this book. See below for British equivalents.

american term	british term
yarn over	yarn over hook (YOH)
slip stitch	single crochet (sc)
single crochet (sc)	double crochet (dc)
half double crochet (hdc)	half treble crochet (htr)
double crochet (dc)	treble crochet (tr)
triple crochet (tr)	double treble crochet (dtr)
double triple crochet (dtr)	triple treble crochet (tr tr)
gauge	tension
skip	miss

gauge

The gauge is the number of stitches and rows over 1 inch of fabric. Many factors affect gauge, including the size of yarn and hook used, the pattern stitch, and even your mood while crocheting. It is important that you measure your gauge correctly (and frequently!) as you work.

To measure your gauge, crochet a piece of fabric at least 5 inches square. Now lay the swatch on a flat surface and count the number of stitches over 4 inches, staying away from all edges of the fabric. Divide that number by 4 to determine your stitch gauge.

If you have fewer stitches per inch than the number specified in your pattern, then switch to a smaller hook; if you have more stitches, then switch to a larger one.

Although it is often less crucial than stitch gauge, your row gauge should be measured the same way.

skill level

In this book, you'll find three different skill levels.
1 = Beginner
2 = Advanced beginner
3 = Intermediate

how to crochet

holding the hook

Hold the crochet hook in your dominant hand, using either the knife (**1a**) or pencil (**1b**) position as illustrated. You might want to try both grips and choose the one that is most comfortable for you.

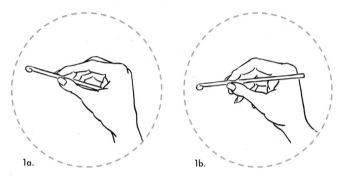

1a.

1b.

slip knot

Begin at least 6 inches from the end of the yarn and make a loop (**2a**), laying it on top of the yarn as it comes out of the ball. Insert your hook into this loop and grab the yarn (**2b**), pulling it slightly to tighten the knot as illustrated (**2c**), adjusting its size to fit the hook while still allowing it to slide easily.

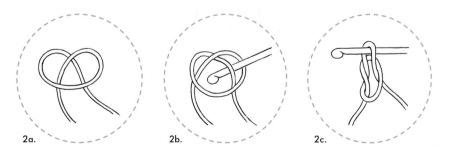

2a.

2b.

2c.

holding the yarn

The way you hold the yarn will affect the evenness of your stitches. Loop the yarn loosely around the index finger of your non-dominant hand, allowing it to trail down your palm, anchored by your last two fingers or wrapped around your little finger. Pinch together your thumb and third finger just below the loop on the hook to hold the work you are crocheting. As you go, be sure to move the anchoring thumb and third finger up every couple of stitches to help you maintain even tension (3).

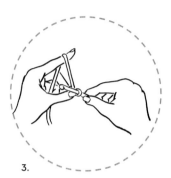

3.

yarn over

Crocheted stitches are formed by wrapping the yarn over the hook and drawing it through loops of yarn already on the hook. When doing the yarn over, *always wrap the yarn from back to front over the hook as illustrated* (4a and 4b), *using the yarn that is over your index finger and closest to the hook.*

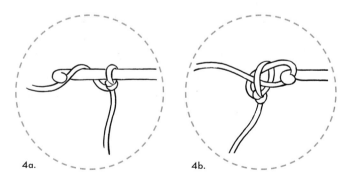

4a.　　　　4b.

basic stitches

chain stitch (ch)

The chain stitch is the base of crocheting. To make a chain stitch, yarn over hook, and draw it through the loop on the hook. Be careful not to crochet too tightly when creating your foundation chains, since successive rows must be worked into the links of the chain.

how to count chain stitches

Each time you yarn over and pull a new loop through the loop on your crochet hook, you are creating one chain stitch. The loop sitting on the hook and the original slip knot never count as stitches or chains (5).

turning-chain

At the end of each row or round, a turning-chain is used to bring the yarn and crochet hook up to the height required for working the next row or round. A row of single crochet stitches, for example, has the same height as a single chain stitch; therefore, when moving from one row of single crochet to another, you must chain one stitch to turn.

In all cases except single crochet, the turning-chain counts as the first stitch of the next row. After chaining three stitches to turn before a row of double crochet, for instance, you would insert your hook into the second stitch of the row; your last double crochet stitch would be worked into the top of the turning-chain-3 at the end of the row.

Refer to the following chart for recommended turning-chain heights:

Crochet Stitch	Corresponding Turning-Chain
Single crochet	Chain one
Half double crochet	Chain two
Double crochet	Chain three
Triple crochet	Chain four
Double triple crochet	Chain five

where to insert your hook

Unless the pattern tells you otherwise, insert your hook under both loops of a chain or stitch (6).

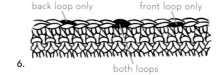

back loop only   front loop only

6.

both loops

slip stitch

Insert the hook into the indicated stitch, yarn over and draw up a loop (two loops are on your hook); immediately pull the new loop through the existing loop on the hook (7).

7.

single crochet (sc)

Insert hook from front to back into indicated stitch, yarn over and pull up a loop (two loops are on your hook; **8a**); yarn over and draw it through both loops on the hook (**8b**).

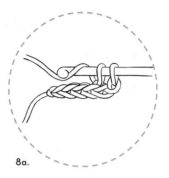

8a.

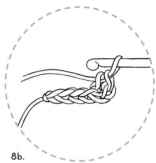

8b.

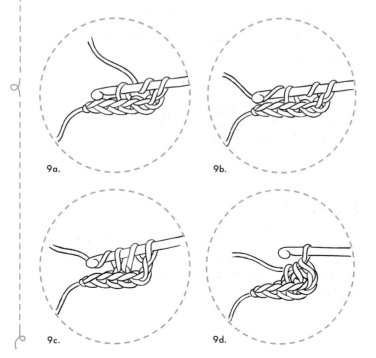

9a.

9b.

9c.

9d.

half double crochet (hdc)

Yarn over, insert hook from front to back into indicated stitch (**9a**), yarn over (**9b**) and pull up a loop (three loops are on your hook; **9c**); yarn over and draw it through all three loops on the hook (**9d**).

double crochet (dc)

Yarn over, insert hook from front to back into indicated stitch, yarn over **(10a)** and pull up a loop (three loops are on your hook; **10b**); yarn over and draw it through two loops on the hook (two loops remain on your hook; **10c**); yarn over and draw it through the remaining two loops on your hook **(10d)**.

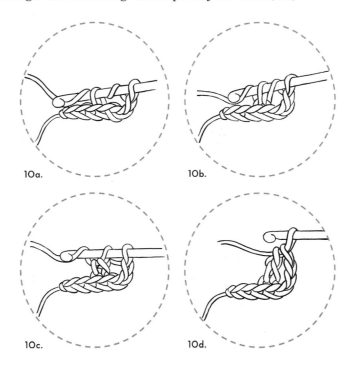

10a.

10b.

10c.

10d.

triple crochet (tr)

Yarn over hook *twice,* insert hook from front to back into indicated stitch (**11a**), yarn over and pull up a loop (four loops are on your hook; **11b**); yarn over and draw it through two loops on the hook (three loops remain on your hook; **11c**); yarn over and draw it through two loops on the hook (two loops remain on your hook; **11d**); yarn over and draw it through the remaining two loops on your hook (**11e**).

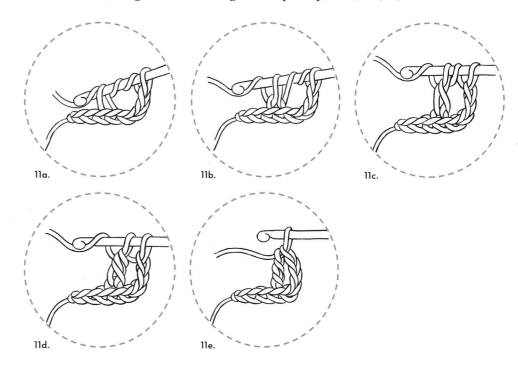

11a.

11b.

11c.

11d.

11e.

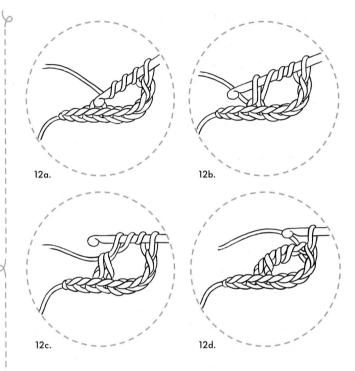

12a.

12b.

12c.

12d.

double triple crochet (dtr)

Yarn over hook *three times* (12a), insert hook from front to back into indicated stitch, yarn over and pull up a loop (five loops are on your hook; 12b); yarn over and draw it through two loops on the hook (four loops remain on your hook; 12c); yarn over and draw it through two loops on the hook (three loops remain on your hook); yarn over and draw it through two loops on the hook (two loops remain on your hook); yarn over and draw it through the remaining two loops on your hook (12d).

taller stitches

Triple triple crochet, quadruple triple crochet, and other tall stitches are made by initially wrapping the yarn around the hook four, five, or even more times, and then working two loops off at a time in the same manner as with double triple crochet stitches.

other techniques

increasing and decreasing

In order to shape your crocheted fabric, you need to increase or decrease the number of stitches in the row or round. You can use different methods for increasing and decreasing stitches, depending on whether the change occurs in the center or at the edge of your fabric:

To increase stitches *in the middle* of a row or round, just work two or more stitches into a single stitch.

To increase a number of stitches *at the edge* of your fabric, make the required number of chain stitches plus some extra ones to comprise a turning-chain (see chart on page 18 for recommended turning-chain heights), and then work directly into them the same way you would a foundation chain.

To decrease stitches *in the middle* of a row or round, combine two stitches into one by working the first stitch until the step in which two loops remain on the hook, and then work the second stitch up to the same step; yarn over hook and draw it through all loops on the hook.

To decrease a number of stitches *at the end* of a row, leave the required number of stitches unworked at the end of a row, make your turning-chain, and turn; to decrease stitches *at the beginning* of a row, work slip stitches over the stitches to be decreased, chain the required number of stitches for height, and begin the new row.

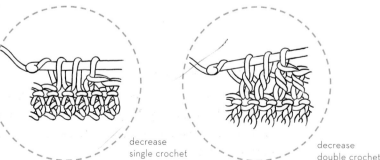

decrease
single crochet

decrease
double crochet

working in the round

Many patterns, such as hats, baby booties, and doilies, are worked circularly. In this type of crochet, the last stitch of each round is connected to the first stitch with a slip stitch, eliminating seams. When you are working in the round, the right side of the fabric is always facing you.

To work in the round, create a foundation chain of the required number of chain stitches. Then make a slip stitch into the last chain from the hook **(13a and 13b)**. Work the required number of stitches into the center of the ring **(13c)**. Usually, rounds are completed by working a slip stitch into the top of the first stitch or chain of the round **(13d)**.

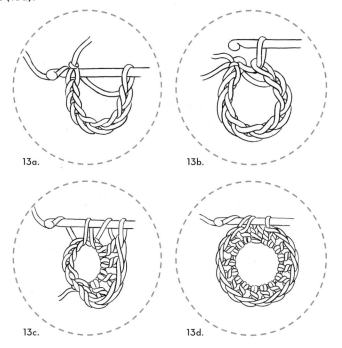

13a.

13b.

13c.

13d.

working into an open ring

Sometimes it is preferable to work around a circle of yarn rather than into a ring of chain stitches. To do so, loop the yarn around your fingers a few times (14a), and then make one chain stitch to connect them (14b). Work the stitches in the loop as above.

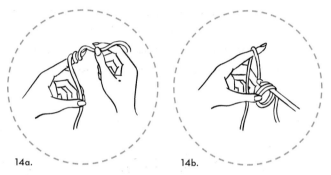

14a.   14b.

working over a ring

To cover a ring with crocheted stitches, as when working over the handles in the Springtime Purse, attach the yarn with a slip stitch, and then work the required number of stitches around the ring as above.

working into back loop only

Sometimes pattern instructions will direct you to work into the back loop only instead of into both loops of a stitch, see illustration on page 18. This technique adds texture to the fabric and is often used to create a ribbed effect.

working around the post of a stitch

Occasionally, it will be necessary to work a stitch around the stem of a stitch in the row below, as in the Hugs and Kisses Baby Blanket on page 103. If, for example, you insert your hook around the stitch from the front to the back to front, the resulting stitch will appear raised on the front of the fabric.

attaching new yarn

To make the joining of new yarn as invisible as possible, try to attach it at the beginning of a row whenever you can. Leaving a 6-inch tail, work the last stitch of the old yarn until two loops remain on your hook; leaving a 6-inch tail, grab the new yarn with the hook and draw it through those two remaining loops to complete the stitch (15). Later, use a tapestry needle to work in those yarn tails (see page 29).

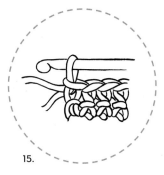

15.

changing color

To change colors as you crochet, work the last stitch of the first color until two loops remain on your hook, and then complete the stitch with the new color, just as you would when attaching new yarn.

crocheting with fabric strips

Using fabric strips instead of yarn creates a cozy, homey effect.
To prepare fabric for crocheting:

1. Cut or tear off selvages.
2. Cut or tear fabric, parallel to the selvage, into strips of the desired width.
3. Join strips by cutting a ¾-inch slit near the end of each strip of fabric, about ½ inch from the edge (16a).
4. With right sides facing up, lay the ends of two separate strips on top of one another, with the slits overlapping (16b).
5. Bring the opposite end of one strip through both slits from bottom to top (16c).
6. Pull strips to form a small knot (16d).
7. After enough strips have been joined together, loosely wind into a ball.

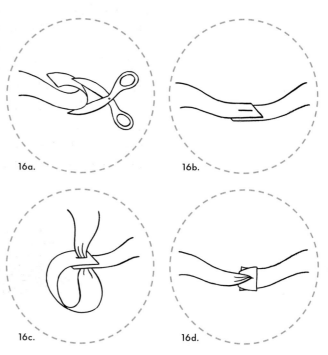

16a.

16b.

16c.

16d.

crocheting with beads

Beads add sparkle to crocheted creations with very little extra effort.

To do a back bead single crochet, follow the steps below.

1. Prestring beads onto your thread or yarn *in reverse order,* with the bead you'll use first strung last.
2. Add a bead during the last step of a crocheted stitch; it should fall to the reverse side of the fabric. For example, to add a bead to a single crochet stitch, insert the hook into the stitch, yarn over hook and draw up a loop (two loops are on your hook), move a bead up next to the two loops, and yarn over hook (17) and draw it through both loops. The bead is now attached to the reverse side of the stitch you just made.

17.

finishing

fastening off

To secure the last stitch in a piece, cut the yarn at least 6 inches from the hook, and draw it through the remaining loop (18).

18.

hiding yarn tails

Using a blunt, wide-eyed tapestry needle, make short running stitches on the wrong side of your fabric in a diagonal line for about an inch or so, piercing the yarn strands that compose the stitches of your fabric. Then, work back again to where you began, working right next to your previous running stitches. Finally, work a stitch or two actually piercing the stitches you just created. Hide each tail individually in opposite diagonal directions, neatly securing your yarn ends while keeping the public side of your fabric beautiful.

sewing seams

Often, you will need to sew pieces of your project together after creating the crocheted fabric. There are many ways of seaming your work, depending on the situation:

The quickest seams are crocheted together using slip stitches or single crochet stitches (19a–19c).

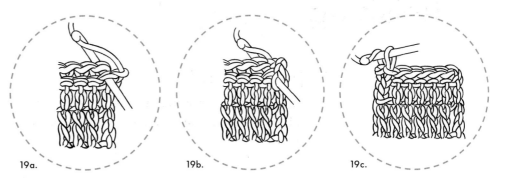

19a.   19b.   19c.

Whipstitched seams are suitable for joining straight pieces of fabric such as square motifs. For a very flat seam, join by stitching through the back loops only (19d).

19d.

Mattress stitch seams are the least visible ones of all and are preferable for garments. These seams are worked using a tapestry needle with the public side of the fabric facing you. The following illustrations show this technique used to join sides of rows together, but the same method can be used to seam tops of rows, too (19e, 19f).

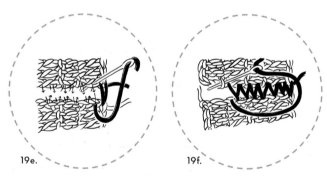

19e.   19f.

blocking

In order to smooth out your fabric and to even out the stitches, block your crocheted pieces prior to seaming them. To do so, first follow the laundering instructions on the yarn label, then spread out the damp fabric on a well-padded surface until it reaches the desired measurements, gently stretching if necessary (using rustless pins!), and allow it to dry. Or, gently steam the fabric into shape by placing a damp cloth over it and carefully running a steam iron just above it.

applying fringe

Simple to make, fringe adds a decorative edge to home decor and fashion items.

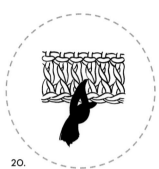

20.

1. Cut a piece of cardboard to your desired fringe length.
2. Wind the yarn around the cardboard several times, and then cut the yarn along the lower edge.
3. With the right side of your fabric facing you, fold several strands of fringe in half and use a crochet hook to loop them onto your project.
4. To secure it, pull the ends of the fringe through the loop (20).
5. Trim fringe evenly.

For ease in finishing, sometimes yarn tails can be incorporated into fringe rather than being woven in. To do this, begin and end leaving tails of at least 6 inches. When adding additional strands of fringe, simply pull the yarn tails through the loop to secure them.

embroidering a French knot

Small touches of embroidery can be used to add decorative details to crocheted fabric, such as the French knots for the eyes of the Mohair Mouse Cat Toy (page 96).

1. Bring the needle up to the right side of the fabric at the spot where you'd like your French knot.
2. Wind the yarn around the point of the needle once, twice, or as many times as you'd like, depending on the desired size of your knot.
3. Insert the needle back through the fabric a short distance from where it emerged from the wrong side.
4. Tighten knot and fasten off.

first projects

everyday dishcloth

skill level 1

Here's our first project: a useful dishcloth composed of only one type of stitch. Perfection isn't an issue here, so just relax and enjoy the process of crocheting!

○ ○ ○ ○ ○ ○ ○ ○ ○ ○ ○ ○ ○ ○ ○ ○ ○ ○ ○ ○

dishcloth

Ch 29.

Foundation Row (RS): Sc into second ch from hook and into each ch across—28 sc. Ch 1, turn.

Row 1 (WS): Sc into first sc and into each sc across—28 sc. Ch 1, turn.

Row 2: Follow instructions for Row 1. Ch 1, turn.

Repeat **Rows** 1 and 2 until piece measures approx 8" from beg, ending after RS row. *Do not fasten off.* Ch 1.

border

Working around dishcloth, counterclockwise, with RS facing: ch 14 for loop, work 30 sc evenly along side edge, 3 sc into corner, work 26 sc evenly along lower edge, 3 sc into corner, work 30 sc evenly along next side edge, 3 sc into corner, work 26 sc evenly along upper edge. Join with a slip st to first sc. Fasten off.

variations: Crocheting a dishcloth provides the perfect opportunity to experiment with interesting stitch patterns. Browse through one of the stitch dictionaries listed on page 119 (they are included in the Instructional Resources), and let the fun begin!

stitches and techniques used

Chain, single crochet, slip stitch

Increasing

Working in the round

materials

Elmore-Pisgah's Peaches & Creme (worsted weight; 100% cotton; each approx 2½ oz/71 g and 122 yd/112 m), 1 ball Mauve #48

Crochet hook, size I/9 (5.50 mm) or size needed to obtain gauge

gauge

In patt, 14 sts and 16 rows = 4". To save time later, check your gauge.

finished size

Approx 8 x 8"

soft coaster

Lots of crocheted patterns are worked in the round, so you'll want to learn the technique right away. Practice while making this quick-to-stitch coaster. Strategically placed increases worked every round keep it flat.

○ ○ ○ ○ ○ ○ ○ ○ ○ ○ ○ ○ ○ ○ ○ ○ ○ ○ ○

coaster

Ch 4.

Rnd 1 (RS): 11 dc into fourth ch from hook. Join with slip st to top of ch-3—12 sts.

Rnd 2: Ch 3. Dc into same st as slip st, *2 dc into next dc. Repeat from * around, ending row with slip st to top of ch-3—24 sts.

Rnd 3: Ch 3. Dc into same st as slip st, *dc into next dc, 2 dc into each of next 2 dc, dc into next dc, 2 dc into next dc. Repeat from * around, ending rnd with dc into next dc, 2 dc into each of the next 2 dc. Slip st to top of ch-3—39 dc.

Rnd 4: Ch 3. Dc into same st as slip st, *dc into next dc, 2 dc into next dc. Repeat from * around. Join with slip st to ch-3—59 sts. Fasten off.

variation: Crocheted at a tighter gauge with finer yarn, this pattern will create wonderful holiday ornaments. Just make a chain, fold it in half, and attach it to the round motif for hanging.

---

stitches and techniques used

Chain, double crochet, slip stitch

Increasing

Working in the round

---

materials

Elmore-Pisgah's Peaches & Creme (worsted weight; 100% cotton; each approx 2½ oz/71 g and 122 yd/112 m), Williamsburg Blue #24 and Chocolate #121; 2 balls will make 4 coasters

Crochet hook, size G/6 (4.50 mm) or size needed to obtain gauge

---

gauge

In patt, Rnds 1 and 2 measure 2" in diameter. To save time later, check your gauge.

---

note

Each dc and ch-3 counts as 1 st.

---

finished size

Approx 4" in diameter

chapter

home decor

classic ripple blanket

Whip up this one-stitch wonder, and you'll have all your friends thinking you're a crochet expert! No one needs to know how quick and easy it was to stitch.

o o o o o o o o o o o o o o o o o o o

stripe pattern

*6 rows A, 2 rows B, 2 rows C, 2 rows B. Repeat from * for patt, ending last repeat with 6 rows of A.

blanket

With A, ch 135.

Foundation Row (RS): Sc into second ch from hook and into next 6 ch, *3 sc into next ch, sc into next 7 ch, skip next 2 ch, sc into next 7 ch. Repeat from * across, ending row with 3 sc into next ch, sc into next 7 ch—136 sc total. Ch 1, turn.

Patt Row: Skip first sc, sc into next 7 sc, *3 sc into next sc, sc into next 7 sc, skip next 2 sc, sc into next 7 sc. Repeat from * across, ending row with 3 sc into next sc, sc into next 6 sc, skip next sc, sc into last sc—136 sc total. Ch 1, turn.

Repeat **Patt Row,** working 136 sc total each row, in Stripe Pattern until blanket measures approx 75" from beg, ending after 6 rows of A. Fasten off.

variation: Can you envision this pattern in a long, ultra-warm scarf? To make one, chain 33 to start. Work the ripple pattern with 34 sc per row until your piece reaches your desired length. Quick and cozy!

stitches and techniques used

Chain and single crochet

Changing color

materials

Lion Brand's Wool-Ease Thick and Quick (bulky weight; all colors 80% acrylic/20% wool except for Wheat #402, which is 86% acrylic/10% wool/ 4% rayon; each approx 6 oz/170 g and 108 yd/99 m), 9 skeins Wheat #402 (A), 6 skeins Fisherman #099 (B), and 3 skeins White #100 (C)

Crochet hook, size N/15 (10.00 mm) or size needed to obtain gauge

gauge

In patt, each ripple measures 7" across. To save time later, check your gauge.

finished size

Approx 56 x 75"

cuddly afghan

You'll get lots of practice making all the common stitches while creating this snuggly afghan. Little triangles nestle together, creating an open yet cozy fabric.

○ ○ ○ ○ ○ ○ ○ ○ ○ ○ ○ ○ ○ ○ ○ ○ ○ ○ ○ ○

stripe pattern

*1 row A, 1 row B. Repeat from * for patt.

afghan

With A, ch 272.

Foundation Row (WS): Sc into second ch from hook, *make triangle, skip next 4 ch, sc into next ch. Repeat from * across. Change color, ch 4, turn.

Row 1 (RS): Sc into top of triangle, *working into next 4 ch along side of triangle, work sc into first ch, hdc into next ch, dc into next ch, tr into next ch, sc into top of next triangle. Repeat from * across to last triangle, ending row with working into next 4 ch along side of triangle, work sc into first ch, hdc into next ch, dc into next ch, yarn over twice, insert hook into last ch of triangle and pull up a loop (yarn over and draw it through 2 loops on hook) twice, yarn over twice, insert hook into last sc and pull up a loop (yarn over and draw it through 2 loops on hook) twice, yarn over and draw it through all 3 loops on hook. Change color, ch 1, turn.

Row 2: Sc into first st, *make triangle, skip next 4 sts, sc into next tr. Repeat from * across, ending row with triangle, skip next 4 sts, sc into top of turning-ch-4. Change color, ch 4, turn.

continued ✈

stitches and techniques used

Chain, single crochet, half double crochet, double crochet, triple crochet

Changing color

Applying fringe

materials

Plymouth's Encore (worsted weight; 75% acrylic/25% wool; each approx 3½ oz/100 g and 200 yd/184 m), 8 balls Steel Blue #9620 (A) and 7 balls Ice Green #801 (B)

Crochet hook, size I/9 (5.50 mm) or size needed to obtain gauge

gauge

In patt, 4 sts = 1" and 2 rows = 1¼". To save time later, check your gauge.

Repeat **Rows** 1 and 2 in Stripe Pattern until piece measures approx 48" from beg, ending after Row 1 of patt. *Do not change color.* Ch 1, turn.

Next Row (WS): Sc into first st, *ch 4, skip next 4 sts, sc into next tr. Repeat from * across, ending row with ch 4, skip next 4 sts, sc into top of turning-ch-4. Fasten off.

finishing

With RS facing, attach additional strands of matching fringe to the 2 shorter sides of afghan. Trim fringe so that it's even.

variation: If your decorating scheme allows for two coordinating afghans in the living room, lucky you! Make the second one just as the first *except* change the Stripe Pattern slightly by starting with 1 row of A, then alternating 2 rows of B with 2 rows of A throughout, and ending the afghan with a single row of A. You'll be amazed at how different the two patterns look!

notes

To make triangle: Ch 5, sc into second ch from hook, hdc into next ch, dc into next ch, tr into next ch.

Beg and end each color with 6" tails; for ease in finishing, these tails will be worked into fringe later.

This afghan is worked sideways.

- - - - - - - - - - - - - - - - - -

finished size

Approx 48 x 68" excluding fringe

down home throw rug

Made out of thick yarn, this rug works up in almost no time at all. And, since fringe is applied later, there's no need to weave in your yarn tails. Finishing is fast and easy!

o o o o o o o o o o o o o o o o o o

stripe pattern

*5 rows A, 1 row B, 5 rows C, 1 row B. Repeat from * for patt.

rug

With A, ch 196.

Foundation Row (RS): Sc into second ch from hook and into next ch, *ch 1, skip next ch, sc into next ch. Repeat from * across, ending row with sc into last ch—195 sts across. Ch 1, turn.

Row 1 (WS): Sc into first sc, *ch 1, skip next sc, sc into next ch-1 sp. Repeat from * across, ending row with ch 1, sc into last sc. Ch 1, turn.

Row 2: Sc into first sc, *sc into next ch-1 sp, ch 1, skip next sc. Repeat from * across, ending row with sc into next ch-1 sp, sc into last sc. Ch 1, turn.

continued ↠

stitches and techniques used

Chain, single crochet

Changing color

Applying fringe

materials

Paton's Shetland Chunky (bulky weight; 75% acrylic/25% wool; each approx 3½ oz/100 g and 148 yd/ 135 m), 6 balls Charcoal #3042 (A), 3 balls Frosted Rose #3425 (B), and 5 balls Deep Plum #3405 (C)

Crochet hook, size K/10.5 (7.00 mm) or size needed to obtain gauge

gauge

In patt, 13 sts and 12 rows = 4". To save time later, check your gauge.

Repeat Rows 1 and 2 in Stripe Pattern until piece measures approx 35"
from beg, ending after 5 rows worked with A. Fasten off.

finishing

With RS facing, attach additional strands of matching fringe to the 2 shorter
sides of rug. Trim fringe so that it's even.

variation: Would you prefer a larger rug? Simple! Just chain 236 for a 4-x-6' finished
size, or chain 392 for 8 x 10'.

notes

Each sc and ch-1 sp counts as 1 st.

*Beg and end each color with 6" tails;
for ease in finishing, these tails will
be worked into fringe later.*

This project is worked sideways.

----

finished size

Approx 35 x 59" excluding fringe

diagonal stripes pillow

Here's a project that uses an interesting construction technique: each piece is made on the diagonal! You begin at one corner with two stitches, then increase one stitch each side every row until you reach the widest point, and then decrease again. (See photograph, page 51.)

○ ○ ○ ○ ○ ○ ○ ○ ○ ○ ○ ○ ○ ○ ○ ○ ○ ○ ○

stripe pattern

2 rows A, 3 rows B, 3 rows A, 8 rows C, *3 rows A, 3 rows B, 3 rows A, 8 rows C. Repeat from * for patt, ending with 3 rows A, 3 rows B, 2 rows A.

pillow piece

(Make 2.)

With A, ch 2.

Row 1 (RS): 2 sc into second ch from hook. Ch 1, turn.

Row 2: 2 sc into each sc across—4 sc total. Change color, ch 1, turn.

Rows 3–38: 2 sc into first sc, sc into each sc across until 1 sc rem in row, ending row with 2 sc into last sc—76 sc total after Row 38. Ch 1, turn.

Row 39: Dec sc to combine first 2 sts, sc into each sc across until 2 sts rem in row, ending row with dec sc to combine next 2 sts—74 sts total. Change color, ch 1, turn.

Repeat last row in Stripe Pattern until 75 rows have been completed—2 sts total in last row. Fasten off.

---

stitches and techniques used

Chain, single crochet

Changing color

Increasing

Decreasing

---

materials

Classic Elite's Zoom (bulky weight; 50% alpaca/50% wool; each approx 1¾ oz/50 g and 52 yd/48 m), 4 hanks Cream #1016 (A), 3 hanks Grey #1003 (B), and 5 hanks Green #1081 (C)

Crochet hook, size K/10.5 (7.00 mm) or size needed to obtain gauge

18" square pillow form

---

gauge

In patt, 3 sc and 3 rows = 1". To save time later, check your gauge.

---

finishing

With WS tog, join pillow pieces tog as follows: attach B with a slip st to any corner, ch 1, *3 sc into corner, 37 sc evenly along next side to corner. Repeat from * around 3 sides, insert pillow form and cont around, ending rnd with slip st to first sc. Fasten off.

variation: To make a matching throw for your sofa, follow the instructions above, increasing 1 stitch every row until you achieve the size you want; then begin to decrease. Add some matching fringe for the perfect finishing touch.

notes

Dec sc = Decrease single crochet = Insert hook into next st, yarn over hook and pull up a loop (2 loops are on your hook); insert hook into next st, yarn over hook and pull up a loop (3 loops are on your hook); yarn over hook and draw it through all 3 loops on hook.

Each sc and dec sc counts as 1 sc.

Pieces are made diagonally.

finished size

Approx 18 x 18"

boxy pillow

Sometimes working in the round can create square shapes, as illustrated in this project. To form nice, neat corners, make 5 double crochet stitches into them. (Also pictured: Diagonal Stripes Pillow, page 48.)

o o o o o o o o o o o o o o o o o o o

stripe pattern

2 rnds *each* of *A, B, C. Repeat from * for patt, ending with 1 rnd A.

pillow piece

(Make 2.)

With A, ch 4. Join with slip st to form ring.

Rnd 1 (RS): Ch 3, 11 dc into ring. Join with slip st to top of ch-3.

Rnd 2: Ch 3, 4 dc into same st as slip st, *dc into next 2 dc, 5 dc into next dc. Repeat from * around, ending rnd with dc into next 2 dc, slip st to top of ch-3. Change color.

Rnd 3: Ch 3, dc into next dc, *5 dc into next dc, dc into next 6 dc. Repeat from * around, ending rnd with 5 dc into next dc, dc into next 4 dc, slip st to top of ch-3.

Rnd 4: Ch 3, dc into next 3 dc, *5 dc into next dc, dc into next 10 dc. Repeat from * around, ending rnd with 5 dc into next dc, dc into next 6 dc, slip st to top of ch-3. Change color.

continued ✈

stitches and techniques used

Chain, single crochet, double crochet

Changing color

Working into ring

Working in the round

materials

Classic Elite's Zoom (bulky weight; 50% alpaca/50% wool; each approx 1¾ oz/50 g and 52 yd/48 m), 6 hanks Blush Pink #1019 (A), 5 hanks White #1016 (B), and 4 hanks Grey #1003 (C)

Crochet hook, size K/10.5 (7.00 mm) or size needed to obtain gauge

18" square pillow form

gauge

In patt, 12 dc and 6 rows = 4". To save time later, check your gauge.

Rnd 5: Ch 3, dc into next 5 dc, *5 dc into next dc, dc into next 14 dc. Repeat from * around, ending rnd with 5 dc into next dc, dc into next 8 dc, slip st to top of ch-3.

Rnds 6-13: Ch 3, cont as established in Stripe Pattern, working dc into each dc around and 5 dc into each corner. At end of each rnd, join with a slip st to top of ch-3. Fasten off.

finishing

With WS tog, join pillow pieces tog as follows: attach B with a slip st to any corner, ch 1, *3 sc into corner, 54 sc evenly along next side to corner. Repeat from * around three sides, insert pillow form and cont around, ending rnd with slip st to first sc. Fasten off.

variation: It's easy to modify this pattern to fit any size pillow form. Simply keep stitching until your piece reaches the desired size, always working 5 dc into each corner dc.

notes

Each dc and ch-3 counts as 1 st.

RS faces you at all times.

- - - - - - - - - - - - - - - - - - - -

finished size

Approx 18 x 18"

country bowl

{2}
skill level

A resourceful crocheter will wrap just about anything around a hook. This lovely bowl is made in the round out of cotton fabric strips. Sure, preparing the materials takes some time, but you'll find that working with such a novel material is exciting. Don't let those stray threads bother you; just trim the bowl when it's finished.

o o o o o o o o o o o o o o o o o o o

bowl

Ch 2.

Rnd 1: 7 Sc into second ch from hook. Join with slip st to first sc. Ch 1.

Rnd 2: 2 Sc into each sc around—14 sc total. Join with slip st to first sc. Ch 1.

Rnd 3: Sc into same st as slip st, *2 sc into next sc, sc into next sc. Repeat from * around, ending rnd with 2 sc into next sc—21 sc total. Join with slip st to first sc. Ch 1.

Rnd 4: Sc into same sc as slip st, sc into next sc, *2 sc into next sc, sc into next 2 sc. Repeat from * around, ending rnd with 2 sc into next sc—28 sc total. Join with sc to first sc. Ch 1.

Rnd 5: Sc into same st as slip st, sc into next 2 sc,*2 sc into next sc, sc into next 3 sc. Repeat from * around, ending rnd with 2 sc into next sc—35 sc total. Join with sc to first sc. Ch 1.

continued ℒ→

stitches and techniques used

Chain, single crochet, double crochet, slip stitch

Increasing

Working in the round

Working with fabric strips

Working through back loop only

materials

100% cotton fabric, 45" wide, approx 3 yd

Crochet hook, size P/16 (11.50 mm) or size needed to obtain gauge

gauge

In patt, 3 sc = 2" and 4 rows = 2". To save time later, check your gauge.

notes

Each sc counts as 1 st.

To prepare, cut fabric into 1"-wide strips.

finished size

Approx 10" in diameter

Rnd 6: Sc into same st as slip st, sc into next 3 sc,*2 sc into next sc, sc into next 4 sc. Repeat from * around, ending rnd with 2 sc into next sc—42 sc total. Join with sc to first sc. Ch 1.

Rnd 7–12: Sc *into back loop only* of each sc around—42 sc total. Join with slip st to first sc. Ch 1.

Rnd 13: Sc into first st as slip st, *ch 3, 2 dc into same sc as last sc, skip next 2 sc, sc into next sc. Repeat from * around, ending rnd with slip st to first sc.

Fasten off.

lower edging

With RS facing and the top of bowl toward you, attach fabric strip with a slip st to any free loop of any sc from **Rnd 7**, and ch 1, work a slip st into the free loop of each sc from **Rnd 7** around, ending rnd with slip st to the first slip st.

Fasten off.

variation: It'd be easy and fun to crochet a round rag rug to coordinate with this bowl. Just work the pattern as given through Rnd 13, and then continue in sc, increasing 7 sc evenly each rnd until it measures your desired size!

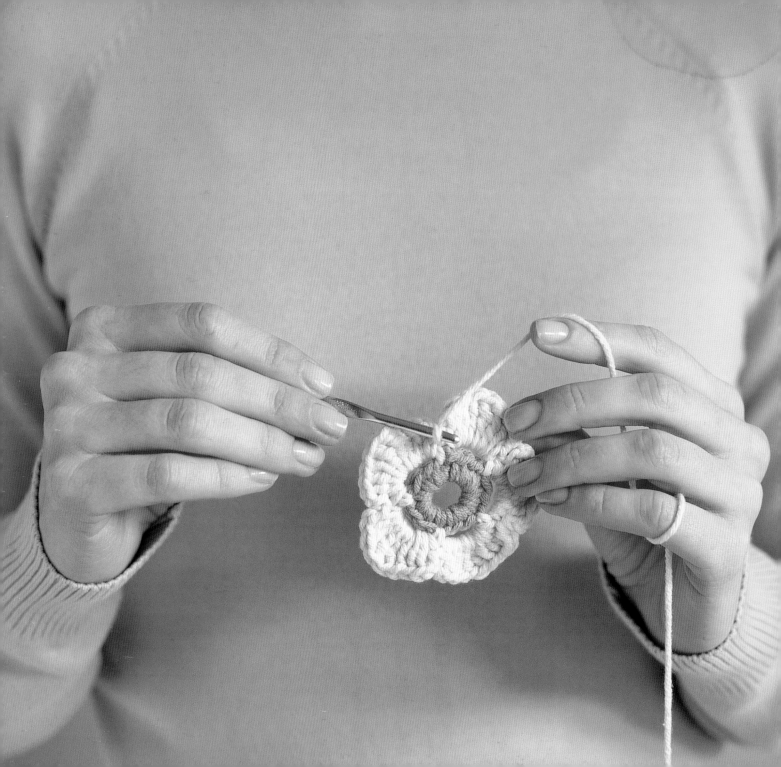

chapter

clothing and accessories

sleeveless shell

This useful shell is elegant and sophisticated. Its subtle texture is created by alternately working into the front and back of stitches.

○ ○ ○ ○ ○ ○ ○ ○ ○ ○ ○ ○ ○ ○ ○ ○ ○ ○

textured pattern

Foundation Row (RS): Hdc into third ch from hook and into each ch across. Ch 2, turn.

Patt Row: Skip first hdc, *hdc *into back loop only* of next st, hdc *into front loop only* of next st. Repeat from * across, ending row with hdc into top of turning-ch-2. Ch 2, turn.

Repeat **Patt Row** for patt.

back

With larger hook, ch 85 (89, 95, 103, 111).

Beg Textured Pattern, and work even on 84 (88, 94, 102, 110) sts until piece measures approx 15" from beg, ending after **WS row**. *Do not ch 2 to turn.*

shape armholes

Turn, slip st into first 4 (5, 6, 7, 8) sts, ch 2, cont in patt as established across next 77 (79, 83, 89, 95) sts. Ch 2, turn, leaving rest of row unworked—78 (80, 84, 90, 96) sts.

Dec 1 st each armhole edge every row 5 (4, 5, 7, 10) times, then every other row 2 (3, 3, 3, 2) times—64 (66, 68, 70, 72) sts rem.

stitches and techniques used

Chain stitch, slip stitch, single crochet, half double crochet, decrease half double crochet

Decreasing

Working into back loop only

Working into front loop only

Sewing Seams

materials

Aurora Yarns/Garnstudio's Muskat (sport weight; 100% Egyptian cotton; each approx 1¾ oz/50 g and 110 yd/100 m), 9 (10, 11, 12, 13) balls Ivory #08

Crochet hook, sizes E/4 (3.50 mm) and F/5 (4.00 mm) or size needed to obtain gauge

gauge

In patt, with larger hook, 20 sts and 12 rows = 4". To save time later, check your gauge.

Cont even until piece measures approx 21½ (22, 22½, 23, 23)" from beg, ending after *W3 row.*

shape neck

Work patt as established across first 16 (17, 18, 19, 20) sts. Ch 2, turn, leaving rest of row unworked. Dec 1 st at neck edge on next row—15 (16, 17, 18, 19) sts rem.

Cont even on this side until piece measures approx 22 (22½, 23, 23½, 23½)" from beg. Fasten off.

for second side of neck

With RS facing, skip middle 32 sts and join yarn with slip st to next st and ch 2. Follow instructions for first side.

front

Follow the instructions for the back until piece measures approx 19½ (20, 20½, 21, 21)" from beg, ending after *W3 row.*

shape neck

Work patt as established across first 21 (22, 23, 24, 25) sts. Ch 2, turn, leaving rest of row unworked. Dec 1 st at neck edge every row 6 times—15 (16, 17, 18, 19) sts rem.

Cont even on this side until piece measures same as back. Fasten off.

continued ⟋→

notes

Each hdc and turning-ch-2 counts as 1 st.

To decrease, work until 2 sts rem in row, then work a dec hdc to combine the last 2 sts in row. On the next row, work last st into the last hdc, not into the top of the turning-ch-2.

Dec half double crochet = Yarn over hook, insert hook into first st and pull up a loop (3 loops are on your hook); yarn over hook, insert hook into next st and pull up a loop (5 loops are on your hook); yarn over hook and draw it through all 5 loops on hook.

- - - - - - - - - - - - - - - - - - ⟋

finished bust measurements

33 (35½, 38, 41, 44)"

for second side of neck

With RS facing, skip middle 22 sts and join yarn with slip st to next st and ch 2. Follow instructions for first side.

finishing

Sew shoulder seams.

neckband

With smaller hook, ch 18.

Foundation Row (RS): Sc into second ch from hook and into each ch across—17 sc total. Ch 1, turn.

Next Row: Sc *into back loop only* of each sc across—17 sc total. Ch 1, turn.

Repeat last row until band, when slightly stretched, fits along neckline. Fasten off. Sew foundation row to last row. Sew side of band to neckline.

Sew side seams.

armhole edging

With RS facing and smaller hook, attach yarn with slip st to upper sleeve seam, and ch 1.

Rnd 1 (RS): Work 71 sc around armhole. Join with slip st to first sc. Fasten off.

variation: For a lighter-weight, crewneck version, omit the ribbed neckband. Instead, work 1 rnd of sc around the neckline.

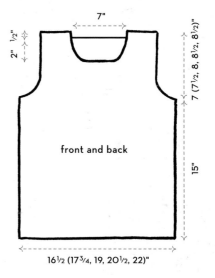

front and back

2" ½"
2"
7"
7 (7½, 8, 8½, 8½)"
15"
16½ (17¾, 19, 20½, 22)"

cozy kerchief

Crocheted head coverings needn't be limited to hats. This triangular kerchief is made from the lowest point up, increasing on each side edge every row. I bet you'll enjoy crocheting shapes other than simple squares and rectangles!

○ ○ ○ ○ ○ ○ ○ ○ ○ ○ ○ ○ ○ ○ ○ ○ ○ ○ ○ ○

kerchief

Ch 4.

Row 1 (RS): Dc into fourth ch from hook. Ch 3, turn.

Row 2: Dc into first dc, ch 2, 2 dc into top of turning-ch-3. Ch 3, turn.

Row 3: Dc into first dc, ch 2, 2 dc into next ch-2 sp, ch 2, 2 dc into top of turning-ch-3. Ch 3, turn.

Row 4: Dc into first dc, ch 2, *2 dc into next ch-2 sp, ch 2. Repeat from * across row, ending row with 2 dc into top of turning-ch-3. Ch 3, turn.

Repeat **Row 4** until piece measures desired size, ending after **RS row.** *Do not fasten off.*

continued ↪

---

stitches and techniques used

Chain, double crochet, slip stitch

Increasing

materials

Coats and Clark's TLC Cotton Plus (worsted weight; 51% cotton/ 40% acrylic; each approx 3½ oz/ 100 g and 186 yd/170 m), 1 ball Tangerine #3252

Crochet hook, size G/6 (4.50 mm) or size needed to obtain gauge

gauge

In patt, (2 dc, ch 2, 2 dc) measures 1" across. To save time later, check your gauge.

note

Each dc and ch-3 counts as 1 st.

finished size

Fits most adults.

ties

Ch 52. Slip st into second ch from hook and into next 50 ch, *slip st into next 2 dc, slip st into next ch-2 sp. Repeat from * across, ending row with slip st into next dc, slip st into top of turning-ch-3. Ch 52, turn. Slip st into second ch from hook and into next 50 ch.

Fasten off.

variation: Turn your mesh kerchief into a full-size triangular shawl! Just continue in the pattern as established until it measures your desired size (or until you run out of yarn!).

flirty skirt

{3}

skill level

*A combination of lots of different crochet stitches makes this skirt as
fun to make as it is to wear!*

○ ○ ○ ○ ○ ○ ○ ○ ○ ○ ○ ○ ○ ○ ○ ○ ○ ○ ○

undulating pattern

Foundation Row (RS): Skip first st, *dc into next st, hdc into next st, sc
into next st, hdc into next st, dc into next st, tr into next st. Repeat from
* across. Ch 1, turn.

Row 1 (WS): *Sc into tr, hdc into dc, dc into hdc, tr into sc, dc into hdc, hdc
into dc. Repeat from * across, ending row with sc into top of turning-ch-4.
Ch 4, turn.

Row 2: Skip first sc, *dc into hdc, hdc into dc, sc into tr, hdc into dc, dc into
hdc, tr into sc. Repeat from * across. Ch 1, turn.

Repeat **Rows** 1 and 2 in Color Sequence for patt.

color sequence

1 row *each* of *B, C, and A. Repeat from * for patt.

back

With A, ch 63 (69, 75).

Foundation Row: Dc into fourth ch from hook and into each ch across—61
(67, 73) sts total. Ch 3, turn.

continued ✐➤

**stitches and
techniques used**

*Chain, slip stitch, single crochet,
half double crochet, double crochet,
triple crochet*

Changing color

Increasing

Sewing Seams

- - - - - - - - - - - - - - - - - ୧

materials

*Aurora Yarn/Ornaghi Filati's Merino
Kind (sport weight; 100% wool; each
approx 1¾ oz/50 g and 137 yd/125 m),
4 (4, 5) balls each Fuchsia #711 (A),
Pink #207 (B), and Rich Plum #226 (C)*

*Crochet hook, size G/6 (4.50 mm) or
size needed to obtain gauge*

Elastic, ¾" wide, cut to fit waist

- - - - - - - - - - - - - - - - - ୧

gauge

*In Undulating Pattern, 15 sts and
10 rows = 4". To save time later,
check your gauge.*

- - - - - - - - - - - - - - - - - ➤

Next Row: Skip first dc, dc into each dc across, ending row with dc into top of turning-ch-3—61 (67, 73) sts total. Ch 3, turn.

Repeat last row until piece measures approx 2" from beg. Ch 4, turn.

Change to B and work **Foundation Row** of Undulating Pattern. Inc 1 st each side every other row 6 times, working new sts into patt as they accumulate—73 (79, 85) sts.

Cont even until piece measures approx 8" from beg.

Cont in patt, and inc 1 st each side every other row 6 more times, working new sts into patt as they accumulate—85 (91, 97) sts.

Cont even until piece measures approx 21" from beg, ending after Row 1 of patt worked with C. Change to A, ch 1, turn.

Next Row (R3): Sc into first 3 sts, *5 dc into next st, sc into next 5 sts. Repeat from * across, ending row with 5 dc into next st, sc into next 3 sts. Fasten off.

front

Follow the instructions for the back.

finishing

Sew side seams.

Fold waistband in half to WS, insert elastic, and *loosely* whipstitch in place.

variations: Would you rather wear a miniskirt? A maxi? It's a cinch to give this colorful skirt your own style. Just continue even in pattern until you reach your desired length. Consider including a side slit, too—just leave one side seam (or both, even) open at the bottom.

notes

Each sc, hdc, dc, tr, turning-ch-3, and turning-ch-4 counts as 1 st.

Pieces are made from the top down.

----

finished hip measurements

45½ (48½, 52)"

----

finished length

20" (excluding edging)

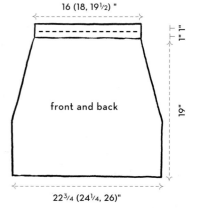

16 (18, 19½) "

1"

front and back

19"

22¾ (24¼, 26)"

springtime purse

You'll love this little bag! Crocheted out of beautiful, hand-painted rayon cord, it's made solely out of single crochet stitches. To begin, you'll work directly onto fun plastic handles. Simple but chic!

front of bag

Row 1: Work 32 sc over 1 ring. Ch 1, turn.

Row 2: 2 sc into first sc, sc into each sc across until 1 sc rem, ending row with 2 sc into last sc. Ch 1, turn.

Row 3: Sc into each sc across. Ch 1, turn.

Repeat last 2 rows 3 more times—40 sc total.

Cont even until piece measures approx 8" from beg. Fasten off.

back of bag

Follow instructions for front of bag.

finishing

Sew sides and bottom of bag, leaving upper 2¼" unsewn on both sides.

variation: Feeling groovy? Apply a bit of fringe along the bottom seam of the bag.

stitches and techniques used

Chain, single crochet

Increasing

Working over a ring

Sewing seams

materials

Judi and Company's Hand-Dyed Cordé (heavy worsted weight; 100% rayon; each approx 5¾ oz/163 g and 144 yd/132 m), 2 hanks Tulip

2 pieces of Judi and Company's PL-9 Plastic Purse Handles, 5" diameter, in Lime

Crochet hook, size F/5 (4.00 mm) or size needed to obtain gauge

gauge

In patt, 16 sts and 16 rows = 4". To save time later, check your gauge.

note

This project is worked from the top down, in two pieces.

finished size

Approx 10 x 8"

halter top

This fun top is composed entirely of little granny squares. Keep some yarn in your purse and whip up a few motifs during your spare moments. You'll have enough to complete the project in no time!

granny square motif

(Make 6 with A, 5 with B, 4 with C, 3 with D, and 3 with E.)

Ch 4. Join with slip st to form ring.

Rnd 1 (RS): Ch 3, 2 dc into ring, (ch 2, 3 dc) 3 times, ch 2, slip st to top of ch-3, slip st into next 2 dc, slip st into next ch-2 sp.

Rnd 2: Ch 3, (2 dc, ch 2, 3 dc) into same ch-2 sp as last slip st, *ch 1, (3 dc, ch 2, 3 dc) into next ch-2 sp. Repeat from * around, ending rnd with ch 1, slip st to top of ch-3, slip st into next 2 dc, slip st into next ch-2 sp.

Rnd 3: Ch 3, (2 dc, ch 2, 3 dc) into same ch-2 sp as last slip st, *ch 1, 3 dc into next ch-1 sp, ch 1, (3 dc, ch 2, 3 dc) into next ch-2 sp. Repeat from * around, ending rnd with ch 1, 3 dc into next ch-1 sp, ch 1, slip st to top of ch-3. Fasten off.

granny half-square motif

(Make 7 with A.)

Ch 4. Join with slip st to form ring.

Row 1 (RS): Ch 3, 2 dc into ring, ch 2, 3 dc into ring. Fasten off.

stitches and techniques used

Chain, double crochet, slip stitch

Working into ring

materials

Classic Elite's Provence (sport weight; 100% cotton; each approx 4½ oz/125 g and 256 yd/233 m), 1 hank each Dark Purple #2652 (A), Bright Purple #2656 (B), Raspberry #2632 (C), Fuchsia #2630 (D), and Pink #2625 (E)

Crochet hook, size F/5 (4.00 mm) or size needed to obtain gauge

gauge

In patt each square measures 2½" across. To save time later, check your gauge.

note

Each dc and ch-3 counts as 1 st.

finished size

Approx 24" wide and 10" long; fits most adults.

Row 2: With RS facing, attach yarn with slip st to top of beg ch-3 of previous row, and ch 3, 2 dc into same ch as slip st, ch 1, (3 dc, ch 2, 3 dc) into next ch-2 sp, ch 1, 3 dc into last dc of previous row. Fasten off.

Row 3: With RS facing, attach yarn with slip st to top of beg ch-3 of previous row, and ch 3, 2 dc into same ch as slip st, ch 1, 3 dc into next ch-1 sp, ch 1, (3 dc, ch 2, 3 dc) into next ch-2 sp, ch 1, 3 dc into next ch-1 sp, ch 1, 3 dc into last dc of previous row. Fasten off.

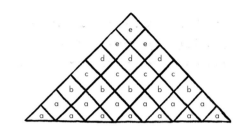

finishing

Arrange motifs according to illustration and, with RS facing, whipstitch them tog through back loops.

lower ties and edging

With A, ch 61. *Work a slip st into second ch from hook and into each ch across. Then, with RS facing, ch 1, work 1 row of sc evenly across lower edge of halter, ch 61, and repeat from * until end of chain. Fasten off.

side edging

With RS facing, join yarn with a slip st to lower corner of halter, and matching colors of squares, work 1 row of sc along diagonal side of halter, working 1 st into each dc and ch-sp. Fasten off.

Repeat for second diagonal edge.

Fold uppermost motif in half and sew it into place on WS.

continued ↪

upper tie

With E, ch 167. Work a slip st into second ch from hook and into each ch across. Fasten off.

Thread upper tie through fold.

variations: For a slightly different (and more modest!) look, crochet your square motifs without holes by working Rnds 1–3 of the Boxy Pillow rather than the traditional granny squares given here. Or, for extra fun, freshen up the mix by including both kinds of motifs, working them in various colors of scrap yarn.

granny squares clutch

skill level 3

You'll find a myriad of uses for this cute clutch bag! Its body is made of fun, textured motifs sewn together, and the top flap is shaped by working partial rows. A simple single crochet edging ties the whole design together, smoothing out any rough edges.

○ ○ ○ ○ ○ ○ ○ ○ ○ ○ ○ ○ ○ ○ ○ ○ ○ ○ ○ ○

motif A

(Make 6.)

Rnd 1 (RS): With A, working into open ring, ch 3, Beg-Popcorn, (ch 3, Popcorn) 3 times, ending rnd with ch 3, slip st to top of ch 3. Fasten off A.

Rnd 2: Attach B with a slip st to any ch-3-sp and ch 3, (3 dc, ch 1, 4 dc) into same ch-3 sp as slip st, *ch 1, (4 dc, ch 1, 4 dc) into next ch-3 sp. Repeat from * around, ending rnd with ch 1, slip st to top of ch-3. Ch 3.

Rnd 3: Dc into next 3 dc, *(dc, ch 2, dc) into next ch-1 sp, dc into next 4 dc, dc into next ch-1 sp, dc into next 4 dc. Repeat from * around, ending rnd with (dc, ch 2, dc) into next ch-1 sp, dc into next 4 dc, dc into next ch-1 sp, slip st to top of ch-3. Fasten off B.

Rnd 4: Attach C with a slip st to any corner ch-2 sp and ch 1, *3 sc into ch-2 sp, sc into next 11 dc. Repeat from * around, ending rnd with slip st to first sc. Fasten off.

motif B

(Make 6.)

Follow the instructions for Motif A, except use the following colors: B for Rnd 1, A for Rnds 2 and 3, and C for Rnd 4.

stitches and techniques used

Chain, slip stitch, single crochet, half double crochet, double crochet

Changing color

Working in the round

Working into open ring

Working into back loop only

Sewing Seams

- - - - - - - - - - - - - - - - - -

materials

Plymouth's Wildflower (sport weight; 51% cotton/49% acrylic; each approx 1³⁄4 oz/50 g and 136 yd/124 m), 2 balls Salmon Pink #80 (A), 2 balls Light Orange #79 (B), and 2 balls Red #63 (C)

Crochet hook, size E/4 (3.50 mm) or size needed to obtain gauge

Fabric for lining

³⁄4" Magnetic snap fastener

Plastic canvas mesh, cut to 9 x 6" (optional, for added stability)

- - - - - - - - - - - - - - - - - -

finishing

With RS facing, using C, whipstitch motifs together though back loops into 4 rows of 3 motifs each, alternating Motif A and B throughout (see illustration, page 76).

top flap

With RS facing, attach C with a slip st to upper RH corner of fabric (see illustration, page 76), and ch 1.

Row 1 (RS): Working *through back loops only,* work 47 sc along top of bag. Ch 3, turn.

Row 2: Skip first sc, dc into next 46 sc. *Turn. Do not ch.*

Row 3: Sc into first dc, hdc into next dc, dc into next 43 dc, hdc into next dc, sc into top of turning-ch-3. *Turn. Do not ch.*

Row 4: Slip st into first sc, slip st into next hdc, sc into next dc, hdc into next dc, dc into next 39 dc, hdc into next dc, sc into next dc. *Turn, leaving rest of row unworked. Do not ch.*

Row 5: Slip st into first sc, slip st into next hdc, sc into next dc, hdc into next dc, dc into next 35 dc, hdc into next dc, sc into next dc. *Turn, leaving rest of row unworked. Do not ch.*

Row 6: Slip st into first sc, slip st into next hdc, sc into next dc, hdc into next dc, dc into next 31 dc, hdc into next dc, sc into next dc. *Turn, leaving rest of row unworked. Do not ch.*

continued ⤳

---

gauge

In patt, each motif measures 3" square. To save time later, check your gauge.

notes

Beg-Popcorn = 4 dc into indicated st; remove hook from loop; insert hook into top of last ch-3 and replace loop onto hook; draw loop through top of ch-3.

Popcorn = 5 dc into indicated st; remove hook from loop; insert hook into first dc made and replace loop onto hook; draw loop through top of first dc.

When making motifs, RS is always facing you.

When making top flap, each turning-ch-3 counts as 1 dc.

finished size

Approx 9 x 6"

Row 7: Slip st into first sc, slip st into next hdc, sc into next dc, hdc into next dc, dc into next 27 dc, hdc into next dc, sc into next dc. *Turn, leaving rest of row unworked. Do not ch.*

Row 8: Slip st into first sc, slip st into next hdc, sc into next dc, hdc into next dc, dc into next 23 dc, hdc into next dc, sc into next dc. *Turn, leaving rest of row unworked. Do not ch.*

Row 9: Slip st into first sc, slip st into next hdc, sc into next dc, hdc into next dc, dc into next 19 dc, hdc into next dc, sc into next dc. *Turn, leaving rest of row unworked. Do not ch.*

Row 10: Slip st into first sc, slip st into next hdc, sc into next dc, hdc into next dc, dc into next 15 dc, hdc into next dc, sc into next dc. *Turn, leaving rest of row unworked. Do not ch.*

Row 11: Slip st into first sc, slip st into next hdc, sc into next dc, hdc into next dc, dc into next 11 dc, hdc into next dc, sc into next dc. Fasten off.

edging

With RS facing and C, work 1 rnd of sc around bag, working 3 sc into each corner to keep the fabric flat. Join with a slip st to first sc. Fasten off.

Cut lining to fit bag, including top flap. Sew lining into place, folding ¼" hems to WS, sandwiching the plastic mesh (if using) in between crocheted fabric and lining fabric. Sew on snap fastener.

With WS tog, fold the motif portion of fabric in half, and whipstitch side seams tog.

variation: To transform your clutch bag into a shoulder bag, whip up a little strap. Just make a chain of your desired length, then work a slip st into each chain across. Sew it on, and you're good to go!

top flap

b	a	b
a	b	a
b	a	b
a	b	a

attach yarn for top flap here

fold bag up here (will become bottom of bag)

lacy evening shawl

I bet you'll be saying "Just one more row and then I'll stop" as you make this shawl. Because each successive row requires fewer stitches than the one before it, you'll be racing along!

o o o o o o o o o o o o o o o o o o o o o

shawl

Ch 284.

Foundation Row (RS): Sc into second ch from hook, *ch 2, skip next 2 ch, 3 dc into next ch, ch 2, skip next 2 ch, sc into next ch. Repeat from * across, ending row with ch 2, skip next 2 ch, 3 dc into next ch, ch 2, skip next 2 ch, slip st into last ch. *Do not ch to turn.*

Row 1 (WS): Turn, and *loosely* slip st into ch-2 sp, slip st into next dc, sc into next dc, *ch 5, skip next dc, skip next ch-2 sp, skip next sc, skip next ch-2 sp, skip next dc, sc into next dc in the middle of 3-dc group. Repeat from * across. Ch 2, turn, leaving rest of row unworked.

Row 2: *3 Dc into center ch of next ch-5 sp, ch 2, sc into next sc, ch 2. Repeat from * across, ending row with 3 dc into center ch of ch-5 sp, ch 2, slip st into last sc. *Do not ch to turn.*

Repeat **Rows** 1 and 2 until only one 3-dc group remains, ending after **Row** 2 of patt. Fasten off.

continued ⟶

stitches and techniques used

Chain, slip stitch, single crochet, double crochet

materials

Lion Brand's Glitterspun (worsted weight; 60% acrylic/27% metallic/ 13% polyester; each approx 1¾ oz/50 g and 115 yd/105 m), 10 balls Onyx #153

Crochet hook, size I/9 (5.50 mm) or size needed to obtain gauge

gauge

In pattern, each 3-dc group measures ½" across. To save time later, check your gauge.

notes

This project is made from the top down.

When making the 3-dc groups in Row 2 of the pattern, be sure to make them under both loops of the middle chain.

finished size

Approx 65" wide and 42" long

finishing

With RS facing, attach yarn with a slip st to upper LH corner of shawl and ch 3. (Dc, ch 3, slip st into last dc, 2 dc) into same place as slip st, skip next row along side of shawl, *(2 dc, ch 3, slip st into last dc, 2 dc) into side of next row. Repeat from * along LH side and up RH side of shawl, working [2 dc, (ch 3, slip st into last dc, 2 dc) 3 times] into middle dc at lower point and also at upper RH corner; working along opposite side of foundation chain along top of shawl, work (2 dc, ch 3, slip st into last dc, 2 dc) into same ch as each 3-dc group of *Foundation Row*, ending rnd with (2 dc, ch 3, slip st into last dc) twice into upper LH, slip st to top of first ch 3. Fasten off.

variation: For a more practical shawl, crochet it out of mohair yarn. It'll be lightweight but toasty warm.

frilly-edged wrap

This pretty wrap is created using light and airy V-stitches. If you work each successive row into the chain-spaces of the previous row rather than in the links of the individual chain stitches, your project will move along very quickly.

o o o o o o o o o o o o o o o o o o

wrap

With larger hook, ch 422.

Foundation Row (RS): V-St into fifth ch from hook, *skip next 2 ch, V-St into next ch. Repeat from * across, ending row with skip next ch, dc into last ch. Ch 3, turn.

Patt Row: Skip first 2 dc, *V-St into next ch-1 sp. Repeat from * across, ending row with dc into top of turning-ch-3. Ch 3, turn.

Repeat *Patt Row* until piece measures approx 26" from beg. Fasten off.

finishing

With RS facing and smaller hook, attach yarn with a slip st to upper LH corner of wrap, and ch 1.

Rnd 1 (RS): Work 806 sc around entire wrap, including 3 sc into each corner. Join with slip st to first sc. Ch 7.

continued ꝫ→

stitches and techniques used

Chain, slip stitch, single crochet, double crochet

Increasing

- - - - - - - - - - - - - - - - - - -

materials

Blue Sky Alpacas' Alpaca & Silk (fingering weight; 50% alpaca/50% silk; each approx 1¾ oz/50 g and 146 yd/133 m), 16 balls Blush #33

Crochet hooks, sizes D/3 (3.25 mm) and E/4 (3.50 mm) or size needed to obtain gauge

- - - - - - - - - - - - - - - - - - -

gauge

In patt, with larger hook, 8 V-Sts measure 4" across and 10 rows = 3" high. To save time later, check your gauge.

- - - - - - - - - - - - - - - - - - -

note

V-St = (Dc, ch 1, dc)

- - - - - - - - - - - - - - - - - - -

finished size

Approx 26 x 68"

Rnd 2 (R3): Slip st into third ch from hook, ch 1, *dc into next sc, ch 4, slip st into third ch from hook, ch 1. Repeat from * around, ending rnd with slip st to third ch of ch-7. Fasten off.

variation: For an extra-special, glamorous shawl, add beads to the border. Prestring beads onto your yarn, then work Rnd 1 of the edging as stated in the patt. For Rnd 2, work 1 sc into each sc around and 3 sc into each corner, attaching a bead to every other stitch. For Rnd 3, work Rnd 2 as given in the original patt. Fasten off.

flower motif appliqué

You'll want to appliqué this flower onto nearly everything: hand-crocheted sweaters, hats, bags, and other fashion accessories. It can be used to add a fun burst of color to purchased items, too!

o o o o o o o o o o o o o o o o o

motif

Ch 8. Join with slip st to form ring.

Rnd 1 (RS): Ch 1, 15 sc into ring. Join with slip st to first sc.

Rnd 2: Ch 1, sc into same st as last slip st, *ch 3, skip next 2 sc, sc into next sc. Repeat from * around, ending rnd with ch 3, slip st to first sc.

Rnd 3: Slip st into next ch-3 sp, *(sc, ch 2, dc, 3 tr, dc, ch 2, sc) into ch-3 sp. Repeat from * around, ending rnd with slip st to first sc. Fasten off.

variation: For a more colorful flower, work Rnd 1 in a contrasting color. The samples shown (opposite) use combinations of Butter #30, Orange #47, and Mango #51.

stitches and techniques used

Chain stitch, slip stitch, single crochet, double crochet, triple crochet

Working into ring

Working in the round

materials

Aurora Yarns/Garnstudio's Muskat (sport weight; 100% Egyptian cotton; each approx 1¾ oz/50 g and 110 yd/ 100 m), 1 ball Mango #51

Crochet hook, size F/5 (4 mm) or size needed to obtain gauge

gauge

In patt, after Rnd 1, motif measures approx 1" in diameter. To save time later, check your gauge.

finished size

Approx 2¼" diameter

scoop neck pullover

{3} skill level

Here's my favorite kind of sweater project. Its textured pattern is oh-so-forgiving! If you lose your place as you're stitching, just remember to make a single crochet stitch into each double crochet stitch, and vice versa. And to keep your stitch count constant, be sure to insert your hook into the second stitch of every row (that turning-chain counts as the first stitch), and finish each row by going into the top of the last row's turning-chain. Count your stitches periodically to make sure you are still on track.

textured pattern

Foundation Row (RS): Sc into third ch from hook, *dc into next ch, sc into next ch. Repeat from * across, ending row with dc into next ch, hdc into last ch. Ch 2, turn.

Patt Row: Skip first hdc, *sc into next dc, dc into next sc. Repeat from * across, ending row with hdc into top of turning-ch-2. Ch 2, turn.

Repeat **Patt Row** for patt.

back

Ch 85 (93, 101, 109, 117).

Beg Textured Pattern, and work even on 84 (92, 100, 108, 116) sts until piece measures approx 3" from beg, ending after **WS row.**

decrease for waist

Cont in patt as established, dec 1 st each side every fourth row 4 times—76 (84, 92, 100, 108) sts rem.

stitches and techniques used

Chain, slip stitch, single crochet, half double crochet, double crochet, decrease half double crochet

Working in the round

Increasing

Decreasing

Sewing Seams

materials

Coats and Clark/Aunt Lydia's Caress (fingering weight; 100% microfiber; each approx 2 oz/57 g and 120 yd/110 m), 14 (15, 16, 17) balls Light Yellow-Green #2236

Crochet hook, size F/5 (4.00 mm) or size needed to obtain gauge

gauge

In patt, 18 sts and 16 rows = 4". To save time later, check your gauge.

Cont even until piece measures approx 9½" from beg, ending after WS row.

increase for bust

Cont in patt as established, inc 1 st each side every fourth row 4 times—84 (92, 100, 108, 116) sts.

Cont even until piece measures approx 13½ (13, 12½, 12, 12)" from beg, ending after WS row. *Do not ch 2 to turn.*

shape armholes

Turn, slip st into first 9 (11, 15, 17, 19) sts, ch 2, cont in patt as established across next 67 (71, 71, 75, 79) sts. Ch 2, turn, leaving rest of row unworked—68 (72, 72, 76, 80) sts.

Cont even until piece measures approx 20½" from beg, ending after WS row.

shape neck

Work patt as established across first 18 (20, 20, 22, 24) sts. Ch 2, turn, leaving rest of row unworked. Dec 1 st at neck edge every row twice—16 (18, 18, 20, 22) sts rem.

Cont even on this side until piece measures approx 22" from beg. Fasten off.

for second side of neck

With RS facing, skip middle 32 sts and attach yarn with slip st to next st and ch 2. Complete same as first side.

front

Follow instructions for back until piece measures approx 19" from beg, ending after WS row.

continued ↝

notes

Each sc, hdc, dc, dec hdc, and turning-ch-2 counts as 1 st.

To decrease, work until 2 sts rem in row, then work a dec hdc to combine the last 2 sts in row. On the next row, work last st into the last hdc, not into the top of the turning-ch-2.

Dec hdc = Yarn over hook, insert hook into first st and pull up a loop (3 loops are on your hook); yarn over hook, insert hook into next st and pull up a loop (5 loops are on your hook); yarn over hook and draw it through all 5 loops on hook.

To increase, work 2 sts into 1 st.

- - - - - - - - - - - - - - - - - -

finished bust measurements
37½ (41, 44½, 51)"

shape neck

Work patt as established across first 22 (24, 24, 26, 28) sts. Ch 2, turn, leaving rest of row unworked. Dec 1 st at neck edge every row 3 times, then every other row 3 times—16 (18, 18, 20, 22) sts rem.

Cont even on this side until piece measures approx 22" from beg. Fasten off.

for second side of neck

With RS facing, skip middle 24 sts and join yarn with slip st to next st and ch 2. Complete same as first side.

sleeves

(Make 2.)

Ch 41 (43, 43, 43, 43).

Beg Textured Pattern, and work even on 40 (42, 42, 42, 42) sts until piece measures approx $1/2$" from beg, ending after *WS row.*

Cont patt as established, inc 1 st each side every other row 0 (6, 10, 16, 18) times, then every fourth row 18 (14, 12, 8, 6) times—76 (82, 86, 90, 90) sts.

Cont even until piece measures approx 21 (20$^{1}/_2$, 21, 20$^{1}/_2$, 20)" from beg. Fasten off.

finishing

Sew shoulder seams.

continued ✐→

neckband

With RS facing, attach yarn with slip st to right shoulder seam and ch 1.

Rnd 1 (RS): Work 108 sc around neckline. Join with slip st to first sc.

Rnd 2 (RS): Ch 1, sc into same st as slip st, *ch 4, slip st into third ch from hook, ch 1, skip next sc, sc into next sc. Repeat from * around, ending rnd with ch 4, slip st into third ch from hook, ch 1, skip next sc, slip st to first sc. Fasten off.

Set in sleeves. Sew sleeve and side seams.

sleeve edging

With RS facing, attach yarn with slip st to lower sleeve seam, and ch 1.

Rnd 1 (RS): Work 40 sc around cuff. Join with slip st to first sc.

Complete by following instructions for neckband.

lower edging

With RS facing, attach yarn with slip st to lower right side seam and ch 1.

Rnd 1 (RS): Work 148 sc around lower edge. Join with slip st to first sc.

Complete by following instructions for neckband.

variation: For a more relaxed look, simply omit the waist decreases and bust increases on the front and back. For a less frilly look, work 2 plain rnds of sc along all edges of sweater.

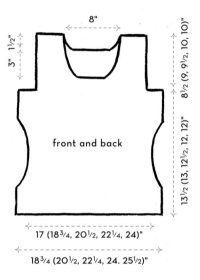

front and back

8"

3" 1½"

8½ (9, 9½, 10, 10)"

13½ (13, 12½, 12, 12)"

17 (18¾, 20½, 22¼, 24)"

18¾ (20½, 22¼, 24, 25½)"

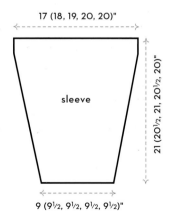

sleeve

17 (18, 19, 20, 20)"

21 (20½, 21, 20½, 20)"

9 (9½, 9½, 9½, 9½)"

hippie belt

Simple enough for advanced beginners, this funky belt is made using just two crochet stitches.

o o o o o o o o o o o o o o o o o o

stripe pattern

1 row each of A, B, C, D, C, B, A.

belt

With A, ch 114 (136, 158).

Foundation Row (RS): Sc into second ch from hook and into next ch, *ch 1, skip next ch, sc into next ch. Repeat from * across, ending row with sc into last ch—113 (135, 157) sts across. Beg with long 25" tail, change to B, ch 1, turn.

Row 1 (WS): Sc into first sc, *ch 1, skip next sc, sc into next ch-1 sp. Repeat from * across, ending row with ch 1, sc into last sc. Beg with long 25" tail, change color, ch 1, turn.

Row 2: Sc into first sc, *sc into next ch-1 sp, ch 1, skip next sc. Repeat from * across, ending row with sc into next ch-1 sp, sc into last sc. Beg with long 25" tail, change color, ch 1, turn.

Repeat **Rows** 1 and 2 in Stripe Pattern until 7 rows have been completed. Fasten off.

continued

stitches and techniques used

Chain, single crochet

Changing color

Applying fringe

materials

Lion Brand's Cotton-Ease (heavy worsted weight; 50% cotton/50% acrylic; each approx 3½ oz/100 g and 207 yd/188 m), 1 ball each Strawberry Cream #101 (A), Bubble-gum #102 (B), Orangeade #133 (C), and Cherry Red #113 (D)

Crochet hook, size H/8 (5.00 mm) or size needed to obtain gauge

gauge

In patt, 18 sts = 4". To save time later, check your gauge.

finishing

With RS facing, attach additional 25" strands of matching fringe to shorter sides of belt.

Work fringe into braids for 3" on each side of belt.

Tie knots to secure braid.

Trim fringe evenly, making each side, including braids, approx 20" on each side of belt.

variations: For a different look, rather than making braids, work a macramé pattern for 3" on each side of the crocheted portion of belt. Or, add chunky beads to the fringed edges.

notes

Each sc and ch-1 sp counts as 1 st.

Beg and end each row with long 25" tails; these tails will become ties.

— — — — — — — — — — — — — — — — — — —⚲

finished size

Approx 25 (30, 35)" long, excluding ties

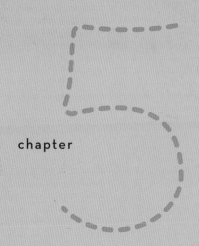

chapter

great gifts galore

mohair mouse cat toy

{2}

skill level

Tired of Kitty playing with your crocheted works-in-progress? Make her a toy of her own! There's no need to buy stuffing—extra bits of yarn will do the trick.

o o o o o o o o o o o o o o o o o

bottom of body

Ch 3.

Row 1 (RS): Sc into second ch from hook and into next sc—2 sc. Ch 1, turn.

Row 2: Sc into each sc across—2 sc. Ch 1, turn.

Row 3: 2 sc into each sc across—4 sc. Ch 1, turn.

Row 4: Sc into each sc across—4 sc. Ch 1, turn.

Row 5: 2 sc into first sc, sc into next 2 sc, 2 sc into last sc—6 sc. Ch 1, turn.

Rows 6 and 7: Sc into each sc across—6 sc. Ch 1, turn.

Row 8: 2 sc into first sc, sc into next 4 sc, 2 sc into next sc—8 sc. Ch 1, turn.

Rows 9–11: Sc into each sc across—8 sc. Ch 1, turn.

Row 12: Sc into each sc across—8 sc. Fasten off.

continued ⤷

---

stitches and techniques used

Chain, slip stitch, single crochet, double crochet, and decrease single crochet

Decreasing

Embroidering French knot

Sewing seams

---

materials

Classic Elite's La Gran (bulky weight; 76½% mohair/17½% wool/6% nylon; each approx 1½ oz/43 g and 90 yd/ 82 m), 1 ball Fuchsia #6541

A small amount of black yarn for eyes

Crochet hook, size H/8 (5.00 mm) or size needed to obtain gauge

---

gauge

In patt, 3 sc = 1". To save time later, check your gauge.

side of body

(Make 2.)

Ch 13.

Row 1 (RS): Sc into second ch from hook and into each ch across—12 sc. Ch 1, turn.

Row 2: Sc into each sc across—12 sc. *Do not ch 1.* Turn. Mark beg of row with a piece of contrasting yarn to indicate tip of nose.

Row 3: Slip st into first 2 sc, ch 1, sc into next 10 sc—10 sc. Ch 1, turn.

Row 4: Sc into first 8 sc—8 sc. *Do not ch 1.* Turn, leaving rest of row unworked.

Row 5: Slip st into first 2 sc, ch 1, sc into next 6 sc—6 sc. Ch 1, turn.

Row 6: Sc into first 6 sc, then work 5 sc evenly along top of rows toward tip of nose, ending row with slip st into last st. Fasten off.

rear of body

Ch 10.

Row 1 (RS): Sc into second ch from hook and into each ch across—9 sc. Ch 1, turn.

Row 2: Dec sc to combine first 2 sc, sc into next 5 sc, dec sc to combine next 2 sc—7 sc. Ch 1, turn.

Row 3: Dec sc to combine first 2 sc, sc into next 3 sc, dec sc to combine next 2 sc—3 sc. Ch 1, turn.

Row 4: Dec sc to combine first 2 sc, sc into next sc, dec sc to combine next 2 sc—3 sc. Ch 1, turn.

notes

Dec sc = Decrease single crochet = Insert hook into next st, yarn over hook and pull up a loop (2 loops are on your hook); insert hook into next st, yarn over hook and pull up a loop (3 loops are on your hook); yarn over hook and draw it through all 3 loops on hook.

Each sc and dec sc counts as 1 sc.

For ease in finishing, beg and end each piece with a 10" tail for use in sewing.

finished size

Approx 4", excluding tail

Row 5: Sc into each sc across—3 sc. Ch 1, turn.

Row 6: Dec sc to combine first 2 sc, sc into next sc—3 sc. Fasten off.

ear

(Make 2.)

Ch 4.

Row 1 (RS): 4 dc into fourth ch from hook. Ch 1, turn.

Row 2: Sc into first 4 dc, sc into top of turning-ch-3—5 sc. Ch 1, turn.

Row 3: Sc into each sc across—5 sc. Fasten off.

tail

Ch 18.

Row 1: Slip st into second ch from hook and into each ch across. Fasten off.

finishing:

Sew first row of sides to side edges along the bottom of body. Sew top of body closed, enclosing extra yarn as stuffing.

Sew rear of body along all three sides.

Sew last row of ear in place, gathering the lower edge slightly.

Sew on tail.

Using contrasting yarn, embroider French knots for eyes (see page 31).

variation: If desired, place some catnip in a plastic bag and tuck it inside the mouse before seaming.

girl's summertime hat

This hat is made in the round, from the top down to the brim. In order to keep your stitch count correct, be sure to end each round with a slip stitch to the first single crochet stitch of the round.

o o o o o o o o o o o o o o o o o o o

hat

Ch 2.

Rnd 1 (RS): 6 sc into second ch from hook. Join with a slip st to first sc. Ch 1.

Rnd 2: 2 sc into each sc around—12 sc total. Join with a slip st to first sc. Ch 1.

Rnd 3: 2 Sc into same st as slip st, *sc into next sc, 2 sc into next sc. Repeat from * around, ending with sc into next sc, slip st to first sc—18 sc total. Ch 1.

Rnd 4: 2 Sc into same st as slip st, *sc into next 2 sc, 2 sc into next sc. Repeat from * around, ending with sc into next 2 sc, slip st to first sc—24 sc total. Ch 1.

Rnd 5: 2 Sc into same st as slip st, *sc into next 3 sc, 2 sc into next sc. Repeat from * around, ending with sc into next 3 sc, slip st to first sc—30 sc total. Ch 1.

Rnd 6: Sc into same st as slip st, sc into next sc, *2 sc into next sc, sc into next 4 sc. Repeat from * around, ending rnd with 2 sc into next sc, sc into next 2 sc. Join with a slip st to first sc—36 sc total. Ch 1.

continued ✈

stitches and techniques used

Chain, single crochet, slip stitch

Increasing

Working in the round

Working into back loop only

materials

Judi and Company's Raffia (heavy worsted weight; 100% rayon; each approx 1½ oz/40g and 100 yd/92 m), 2 hanks Straw

Crochet hook, size I/9 (5.50 mm) or size needed to obtain gauge

gauge

In patt, 3 sc = 1". To save time later, check your gauge.

note

Each sc counts as 1 st.

finished size

Fits most girls, ages 7 to 12.

Rnd 7 : 2 Sc into same st as slip st, *sc into next 5 sc, 2 sc into next sc. Repeat from * around, ending rnd with sc into next 5 sc, slip st to first sc—42 sc total. Ch 1.

Rnd 8 : Sc into same st as slip st, *2 sc into next sc, sc into next 6 sc. Repeat from * around, ending rnd with 2 sc into next sc, sc into next 2 sc, slip st to first sc—48 sc total. Ch 1.

Rnd 9 : 2 Sc into same st as slip st, *sc into next 7 sc, 2 sc into next sc. Repeat from * around, ending rnd with sc into next 7 sc, slip st to first sc— 54 sc total. Ch 1.

Rnd 10 : Sc into same st as slip st, sc into next 4 sc, *2 sc into next sc, sc into next 8 sc. Repeat from * around, ending rnd with 2 sc into next sc, sc into next 3 sc, slip st to first sc—60 sc total. Ch 1.

Rnd 11–18 : Sc *into back loop only* of each sc around—60 sc total. Join with a slip st to first sc. Ch 1.

Rnd 19 : Sc *into back loop only* of same st as slip st, sc *into back loop only* of next 2 sc, *2 sc *into back loop only* of next sc, sc *into the back loop only* of next 3 sc. Repeat from * around, ending rnd with 2 sc *into the back loop only* of next sc, slip st to first sc—75 sc total. Ch 1.

Rnd 20 : Sc *into back loop only* of each sc around—75 sc total. Join with a slip st to first sc. Ch 1.

Rnd 21 : Sc *into back loop only* of same st as slip st, sc *into back loop only* of next 3 sc, *2 sc *into back loop only* of next sc, sc *into the back loop only* of next 4 sc. Repeat from * around, ending rnd with 2 sc *into the back loop only* of next sc, slip st to first sc—90 sc total. Ch 1.

Rnds 22–24 : *Sc *into back loop only* of next sc. Repeat from * around, ending rnd with slip st to first sc—90 sc total. Ch 1.

Rnd 25 : Sc *into back loop only* of each sc around—90 sc total. Join with a slip st to first sc.

Fasten off.

variation: For a winter version of this hat, choose a chenille or wool yarn rather than raffia. Be sure to crochet at a tight gauge so the fabric will keep its shape!

hugs and kisses baby blanket

Here, some stitches are crossed over other stitches to create a beautiful textured fabric. And don't worry about all the yarn tails involved in working the two row stripes: for ease in finishing, don't cut yarn at the end of each section. Instead, carry the yarn loosely up the side of the blanket until you need it again!

○ ○

blanket

With A, ch 146.

Foundation Row (RS): Sc into second ch from hook and into each ch across. Ch 3, turn.

Row 1 (WS): Skip first sc, *dc into next sc. Repeat from * across. Change to B, ch 1, turn.

Row 2: Sc into first 3 dc, *skip next 2 sts, FPDTR into next st two rows below, sc into next dc, FPDTR into skipped st two rows below, sc into next 5 dc. Repeat from * across, ending row with skip next 2 sts, FPDTR into next st two rows below, sc into next dc, FPDTR into skipped st two rows below, sc into next 2 dc, sc into top of turning-ch-3. Ch 3, turn.

Row 3: Skip first sc, *dc into next sc. Repeat from * across. Change to A, ch 1, turn.

continued ✈

stitches and techniques used

Chain, slip stitch, single crochet, double crochet, front post double triple crochet (FPDTR)

Changing color

- ⚲

materials

Paton's Look at Me (sport weight; 60% acrylic/40% nylon; each approx 1³/₄ oz/50 g and 152 yd/139 m), 8 balls Green Apple #6362 (A) and 9 balls Pale Yellow #6353 (B)

Crochet hook, size G/6 (4.50 mm) or size needed to obtain gauge

- ⚲

gauge

In patt, 16 sts and 12 rows = 4". To save time later, check your gauge.

- ⚲

finished size

Approx 36 x 45" excluding border

Row 4: Sc into first 7 dc, *skip next 2 sts, FPDTR into next st two rows below, sc into next dc, FPDTR into skipped st two rows below, sc into next 5 dc. Repeat from * across, ending row with sc into next sc, sc into top of turning-ch-3. Ch 3, turn.

Repeat Rows 1–4 for patt until piece measures approx 45" from beg, ending after Row 4 of patt. Ch 1, turn.

Next Row (WS): Sc into each st across.

Change to B, ch 1, turn.

finishing

Rnd 1 (RS): With B, work 144 sc along upper edge of afghan, 4 sc into corner, 190 sc along left side of afghan, 4 sc into corner, 144 sc along lower edge of afghan, 4 sc into corner, 190 sc along right side of afghan, 4 sc into corner. Join with slip st to first sc. *Do not turn.*

Rnd 2 (RS): Ch 6, slip st into third ch from hook, dc into last sc from Rnd 1, *skip next sc, (dc, ch 3, slip st into third ch from hook, dc) into next sc. Repeat from * around. Join with slip st to third ch of ch-6. Fasten off.

variation: Feeling thrifty? Work this pattern with bits of scrap yarn left over from previous projects, working 2 row stripes of lots of different colors. Just make sure the yarns you use have the same laundering instructions.

vintage-style necklace

Don't you deserve some new jewelry? Make it yourself by crocheting beads onto flexible craft wire! Be sure to take your time, though, since it is difficult to rip out stitches once they're made with these materials.

○ ○

medallion

Prethread all 24 beads onto wire.

Rnd 1: Working into open ring, (sc, ch 3) 12 times, ending rnd with slip st to first sc, slip st into next ch-sp. Ch 1.

Rnd 2: Bb-sc into same ch-sp as slip st, *ch 4, bb-sc into next ch-3 sp. Repeat from * around, ending rnd with slip st to first bb-sc, slip st into next ch-sp. Ch 1.

Rnd 3: Bb-sc into same ch-sp as slip st, *ch 5, bb-sc into next ch-4 sp. Repeat from * around, ending rnd with slip st to first bb-sc, slip st into next ch-sp.

Fasten off.

variation: Transform some pretty beads and silver wire into glittery earrings. Just work Rnds 1 and 2 of the medallion pattern, fasten off, and then attach some purchased earring wires. Use faceted Czech glass beads for extra sparkle!

stitches and techniques used

Chain, slip stitch, single crochet, back bead single crochet

Working into open ring

Working in the round

Crocheting with beads

materials

Glass beads (4 mm), 24 total

Metal wire, 28- or 30-gauge (30 yd/ spool), 1 spool silver

Crochet hook, size B/1 (2.25 mm) or size needed to obtain gauge

Colored cord

gauge

In patt, Rnds 1 and 2 measure ¾" in diameter. To save time later, check your gauge.

finished size

Approx 2" diameter